THE HYPOTENUSE

THE HYPOTENUSE

An illustrated scientific parable
for turbulent times

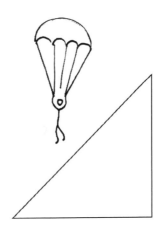

Carlos E. Puente

To Pope John Paul II
In Memoriam

Contents

"A voice of one crying out in the desert:
'Prepare the way of the Lord,
 make straight his paths.
Every valley shall be filled
 and every mountain and hill shall be made low.
The winding roads shall be made straight,
 and the rough ways made smooth,
and all flesh shall see the salvation of God.'"

from The Preaching of John the Baptist

Luke 3:4–6

Preface

In a world in which one out of seven people (that is, 925 million brothers and sisters as of 2010) live in hunger, roughly 50% of the people survive on less than $2.50 a day, and at least 80% of humanity lives on less than $10 a day, this parable has been relaunched in the hopes of contributing to better understand the ultimately simple multiplicative effects that give rise to the universal troubles we all face — troubles that surely cannot be resolved without our collective concerted actions.

In a day and age when citizens all around the world are becoming increasingly aware of wealth and income inequalities, resulting in cries against the wealthiest 1%, I do hope this work would serve as a reminder of the loving blueprint available to us — irrespective of the 99% or 1% side — so that we all may truly address the real issues that divide us with due dignity, harmony, and peace.

This version of the parable is almost identical to the original, save for a few improvements; in particular, an explanation of the sought-after solution has ascended from an obscure footnote to its own section, located just after the Postlude.

Davis, December 8, 2011
On the Feast of the Immaculate Conception of Mary

Preface to the First Edition

Undoubtedly, we live in turbulent times. After enduring in the twentieth century wars and rumors of wars, holocausts, famines, terrorism, corruption, market crashes, drug use, and widespread poverty, humanity already appears destined for more of the same in the new millennium. Despite the best intentions of many, power struggles throughout the world continue to tear the delicate fabric of unity, leading many to hopelessness and indifference. Sadly, as mankind grows older, genuine peace continues to be elusive.

Besides our struggles, the last century has also witnessed advances in science and technology, that have transformed the way we live. Lately, such knowledge has resulted in a host of ideas aimed at understanding and predicting nature's complexity, and in particular that generated by turbulence. This work shows how such ideas provide an impartial framework for visualizing the dynamics and consequences of mankind's divisive traits, which, in a logical manner and consistent with ancient wisdom, points us to a state of balance and friendship, symbolized by the hypotenuse of a right-angled triangle, where we all may achieve peace.

It is my hope that this piece may help raise awareness about the universal nature of the evils we face and may inspire concerted action so that we all may enjoy a truly loving world.

Davis, August 15, 2005
On the Feast of the Assumption of Mary

Prelude

This story is based on a set of simple mathematical constructs known as multiplicative cascades, which progressively divide and redistribute an initially constant object. The parable is set up by following the evolution of generic cascades while realizing that their dynamics uncannily represent mankind's common superiority (or inferiority) attitudes, leading us to "turbulence" at various scales: ourselves, our personal relationships, our communities, our countries, and the world at large.

The narrative is arranged into four main sections—history, math, physics, and common sense, all "bite-sized"—and adopts the format of a picture book with "people" walking on top of mathematical diagrams to help explain the central ideas. In an attempt to reach a wider audience, technical details have been omitted from the main text and collected in a set of notes in the back. The reader may skip the notes on a first reading but is strongly advised to consider them later on, for aside from pertinent references, they include helpful information that clarifies and further establishes the message.

As a corollary to the narrative, the story includes a postlude and a section that further explains the solution to our problems. The parable concludes with three poems-songs: "The Hypotenuse," "609," and "$Y = X$."

A bit of history...

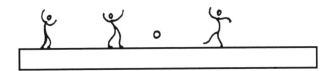

Once upon a time, but not too long ago, simplicity reigned, equilibrium ruled, and life was paradise. People listened, and they could move freely from one place to another, for everything was shared.

Then, some were deceived by a subtle lie. They thought there was a better way—that they deserved more than others—so they selected their friends and disrupted life's normal landscape by cutting it at 70%.

As shall become apparent later on, the choice of 70% is not arbitrary.

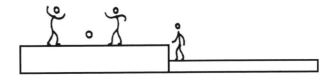

They piled up the largest side on the first half for themselves, and let the others have the smallest piece, stretched on the second half.[1]

As time went on, the same process was repeated on each side along the same proportions. The space was thus divided into four parts holding, in order from left to right,

49% *(70% of 70%)*,
21% *(30% of 70%)*,
21% *(70% of 30%)*, and
9% *(30% of 30%)*

of the resources.[2]

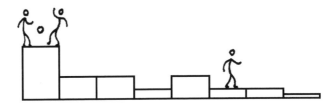

Soon, as competition became established, there arose eight groups arranged into four layers.[3] Life at the top was good, but travel and communications became increasingly difficult, because the vertical distances kept on growing.

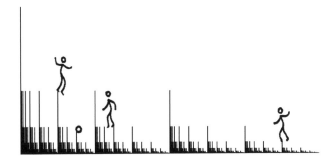

As the **cascade** of division continued, the increased fragmentation gave rise to a great many small segments, even as small as individuals, whose resources were arranged in a repetitive and intertwined fashion.[4]

The vertical scale of the graph for a chain containing only 12 levels of the lie is already more than 56 times higher than the one at equilibrium. While the graph here has been compressed so that it may fit on the page, the people are enlarged so that they do not appear as ants.[5]

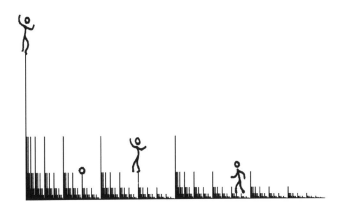

Sadly, this inequitable chain produced unde-
sirable solitude and ample distrust. It also resulted in huge disparities, as the majority of
wealth became concentrated in only a few iso-
lated **thorns**.

*For example, after 16 levels of the lie, the rich-
est 20% of the population owns approximately
80% of the resources — a commonly quoted fig-
ure in discussions of wealth inequalities.*[6]

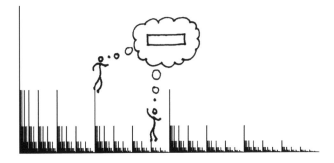

As imbalances grew, the inevitable happened. Rebels, in some highly skewed nations, decided to restore dignity and equality by means of turbulent force.

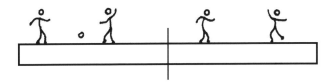

Here, another lie, as subtle as the first one, de-
luded many. Leaders thought that individual
life had no value compared to the state's good.
This belief led them to break the sought model
by the middle.

So that by evenly redistributing the landscape left and right, the voices of disagreement, here allegorically confined to the middle third, would no longer participate in the game of life.[7]

As shall be appreciated later on, the exact choice of the hole size and its placement in the center do not affect the message of the parable.

As forced equality evolved, its implementation led to further isolation of dissenting views and additional emptiness in the fabric of such societies. Sadly, people's distrust and fear multiplied as they moved upwards in the "common landscape."

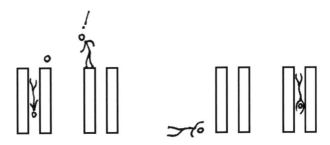

Inevitably, and as it happened with the first lie, unity and friendship crumbled with the passage of time. Many individuals were simply dismissed by this discriminating cascade, and as before, the effective distance between people increased.[8]

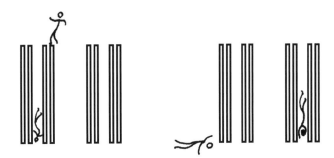

In the end (not shown, to spare our younger readers the horror of nightmares), these states became rather poor, for their intrinsic division left their people, if not exactly their resources, concentrated in equal thorns over **dust**, that is, their society lost its cohesion and became so scattered as spikes that do not touch.[9] Unexpectedly (but in fact quite predictably), there eventually came a day when some of these sand castles collapsed.

When this chain is carried only 12 levels, the height of the resulting rectangles is already more than 129 times higher than the one at equilibrium.[10]

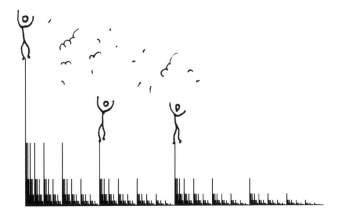

For years, the question had been "Which cascade shall govern the world?" The failure of the
common experiment was hailed as a triumph
by many leaders worldwide, who declared that
their way of life was the greatest on the face of
the earth.

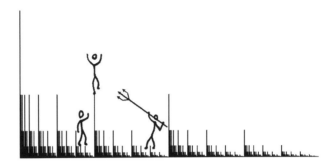

Although many embraced these grandiose assertions, citizens of the world, both within and outside those elite societies, realized that the first lie was not the paradise as they had been told. For the increasingly materialistic rat-race of modern life is not necessarily as good as it gets, for it often brings violence and misery even to those who "win."

Strikingly, a simple cascade with 20 levels using the partitions as before closely fits the skewed wealth distribution in the **United States**.[11]

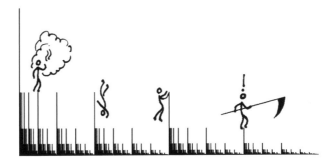

For despite people's good intentions and scientific advances, the inherently selfish game that maximizes profit gives birth to insurmountable walls that obscure the light of love, leading many brethren to escape their "walking in thorns" via a variety of hallucinogens and other worldly distractions.[12]

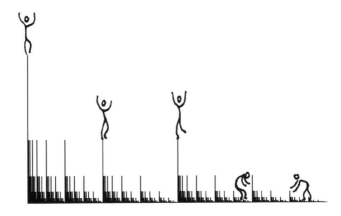

Prospects for the future are daunting, for the winning cascade contains, by layers, the same disconnected organization of the fallen thorns.[13] If the predominant enterprise does spread globally as planned, those with more will surely have even more, those with less even less, and there will be emptiness and dust everywhere...[14]

The vertical scale for a chain containing only 30 levels is already more than 24,201 times higher than the one at equilibrium.

A bit of math...

0   x 1

To further appreciate the subtleties of both lies, it is convenient to consider their "accumulated wealth" as one crosses over their implicit landscapes from left to right, from the beginning to an arbitrary point x.

As shown here for the discriminating cascade, from zero up to $x = 1/3$ there are 50% of the resources, and so it happens up to 2/3, for there is nothing in the middle third.

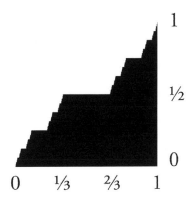

When the accumulated wealth is portrayed as a function of x, the diagram above is found. Such set has great many plateaus which correspond to the gaps where there are no resources at all.

For example, the flat region at wealth one-half comes from the hole from one-third to two-thirds in the previous page, and so on from subsequent holes.

This object is rather peculiar, for if one were to parachute on it, one would think that it is flat upon landing.[15] As the terrain is locally horizontal everywhere, the length of such a rugged boundary, from bottom to top, equals **2** units, that is, one horizontal unit for all the plateaus, plus one vertical unit, as the resources add up to 100%.[16]

This set, due to its curious deceit that makes it appear stable and constant as equilibrium, is known in science as the **devil's staircase**. Other such staircases are found whenever holes of **any** size propagate, that is, any positive size other than one-third.[17]

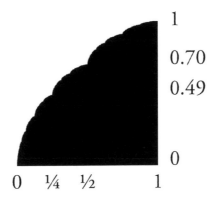

For the inequitable cascade, the accumulated wealth yields the pattern above, with the great many notches reflecting the chain of pile-ups and stretches.

For example, 70% of the accumulated resources happen from zero to $x = 1/2$, the most notorious dent, 49% of them up to 1/4, and so on.

As the notches everywhere turn out to be horizontal-vertical stairs, the actual length of the "cloud" obtained, one that eerily resembles the one seen on a massive explosion, also equals 2 units from bottom to top.

This object is also locally flat, as the tacit lie literally disintegrates all resources everywhere. It is another devil's staircase, and it happens when other imbalances, of **any** size, persist.[18]

When there are neither imbalances nor holes, that is, when the proverbial "fifty-fifty" is attained, the lies are avoided and equilibrium is maintained.

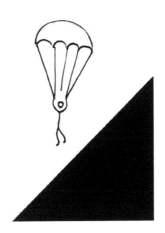

This ideal condition gives rise to an accumulated wealth profile joining linearly bottom and top, that yields the **smallest** distance of

$$\sqrt{2} \approx 1.4142\ldots,$$

in virtue of the famous Pythagorean theorem.

At equilibrium, 50% of the resources are located from $x = 0$ to $x = 1/2$, and 25% of them from $x = 0$ to $x = 1/4$, etc.

While equilibrium ventures straight through the **hypotenuse**, the two cascades ultimately roam by crooked paths that are as long as the **legs** of a right triangle, irrespective of their imbalances and holes. While the genuine balance of friendship follows the most economic path, the two lies wander, in their implacable prejudice, not only greater but maximal lengths.[19]

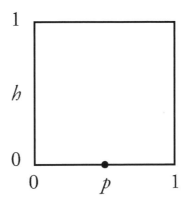

When the two dividing notions are combined to build additional cascades containing both imbalances, p, and holes, h, as we humans often do in our lives, other more exotic sets of thorns over dust and subsequent devil's staircases are produced.[20] As seen here, there is only a **single point**, within a square of possibilities, that leads to the minimal distance of $\sqrt{2}$.

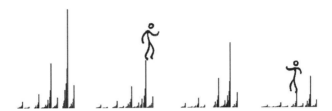

But the picture is even more dramatic, for equilibrium can be fractured into more than two pieces and the sizes of imbalances and holes may be selected randomly from time to time. This general mechanism, which further reflects and encompasses our ever-changing attitudes, would still result in thorns that concentrate in dust.

As before, the diagram here is compressed and the people enlarged, for the vertical scale of the graph for this example containing only 8 levels is already more than 51 times higher than the one at equilibrium.

Such a landscape would invariably give a locally flat and twisted accumulated wealth frontier of maximal length, that is, another devil's staircase, an appropriate name given the chain of divisive traits that produced it.

A bit of physics...

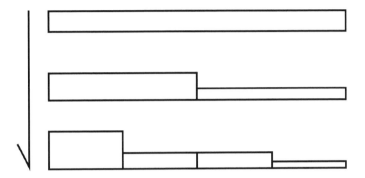

Technological advances in recent years have allowed identifying the progressive breaking, precisely by 70%, in the often-violent scattering process performed by the power of the air.[21]

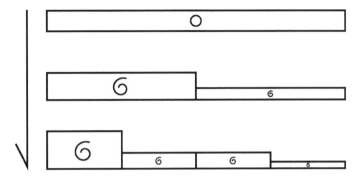

When the air's energy exceeds a threshold, its internal cohesion is shattered, and it flows in an irregular and intermittent fashion known as fully developed turbulence.[22] What one observes is universally consistent with a cascade of inwardly rotating **eddies** that divide into progressively smaller ones and carry distinct quantities of energy (areas above) distributed precisely as in the first lie.[23]

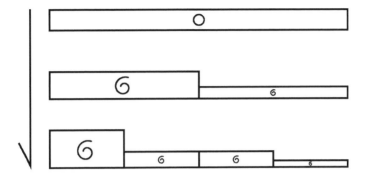

This natural condition, guided by the allegorical ratio $2/3 = 0.666\ldots$,[24] is rather common in the world.[25]

In the end, turbulence **dissipates** all its energy via the smallest eddies, and all its thorny outbursts simply disintegrate as heat and bankrupt themselves like dust,[26] to restart yet another cycle of eddies and violence later, when possible.

A bit of common sense...

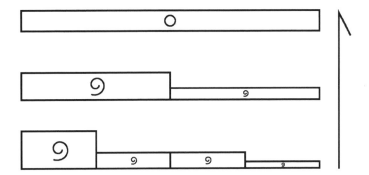

As the upheaval and demise of natural turbulence occurs in consonance with a simple cascade, we may learn from such a generic notion
to **rectify** and hence avoid "biting the dust."
For although a bit of turbulence may be good to
shape our characters, it is wise to slow down to
escape being trapped by the destructive eddies.

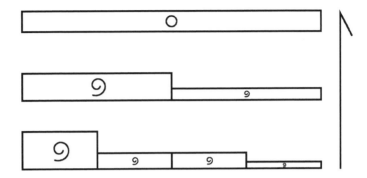

Clearly, it is all a matter of choices, for we can discipline ourselves to live below "the threshold" and "change the wind" to sail the natural cascade in reverse, cutting the mountains and filling the valleys, repairing the breach, in order to restore **unity**.[27] For in a rather vivid way, $1 = 0.999\ldots$.[28]

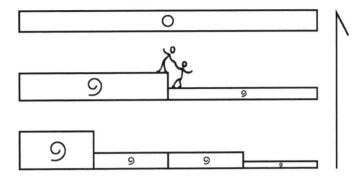

For we may tap our moral energy to turn the inward, selfish, and negative spiral into an outward, loving, and positive one,[29] hence evading the predicted darkness existing between 6 and 9.[30] For while the divisive eddy seeks vengeance of the finite past, the humble one forgives as it dreams of forever.[31]

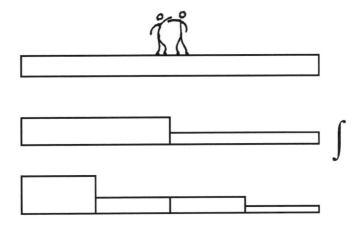

For we, having been endowed with a soul, can transform violence into calmness, indifference into compassion, solitude into friendship, and the corrupting illusion induced by our desire of wealth ($) into its opposite, the slender S of brotherly integration, empowering us to conduct, rather than to dissipate, the flame of life.

As we savor during our quiet times, there is only one common high ground for internal and external **peace**, only one stable solution that we can walk freely without fear of stumbling, only one case that allows transparent communication among all people: the elusive but real condition without thorns and holes.

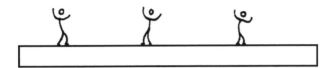

As there is essentially $\sqrt{2}$ or 2, integrity or multiple dust, there is only one **radical** and solid foundation that ensures our survival rather than our annihilation;[32] only one strategy that restores dignity and justice to all; only one that, by being truthful, respects all life and heals all wounds.[33]

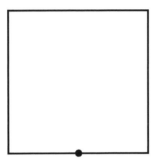

As this ideal, feasible condition is but a needle in a haystack, this realization pierces our egos, for it reminds us of how easy it is to "miss the point" and be **hypocritical**. For it is much easier to blame others than to recognize our own faults, to respond to violence with violence than to offer the other cheek, to forget one's essential dream than to dare to forge it, lest we end up beheaded or crowned with thorns.[34]

The key is then in courageously exchanging the imaginary and impossible, that is, the root of the negative, into the improbable but real, that is, the positive root of the positive,[35] so that all of us, sharing our diverse talents and sincere hearts, may accept the unitive power of self-sacrifice to take refuge in the practical and precious hypotenuse, given by the simplest of equations $\mathbf{Y} = \mathbf{X}$.[36]

For the invitation is eternal and rather plain. We should listen again to realize our ultimate hope, so that in all intelligence and humility, that is, in the fullness of **Love**, we, all the citizens of the world, may weave a secure home land and play together at last.

Postlude

This parable represents an urgent plea for equality, unity, and love, in the midst of ample "turbulence" in the world today. It is urgent for more reasons than one. Obviously, many brothers and sisters worldwide presently lack the essential means for their survival. Moreover, the laws of physics warn us of the generalized collapse looming if we allow thorns to cascade and perpetuate in our increasingly interconnected world.

Before us, embodied in the serenity of equilibrium and in the intrinsic justice of the one-to-one line, lies the clear antidote to our anxieties and fears, the all-encompassing relief of the widespread evils of selfishness, corruption, and greed that have plagued mankind's hearts since ancient times. Before each one of us lies, individually and collectively, the conscious task of building a civilization of love, restoring human dignity, admitting and mending mistakes, freely sharing resources and talents, and truly choosing world peace above world war.

In an age when the fear of terror naturally suggests military and/or economic solutions to the evils of our world, it is sober to realize that the best road map for prosperity and mass construction has always been the globalization of love. For, as supported by modern science and reaffirmed by common sense, only in the gracious simplicity of the hypotenuse can we all achieve real freedom and lasting peace.

Now someone approached him and said, "Teacher, what good must I do to gain eternal life?" He answered him, "Why do you ask me about the good? There is only One who is good. If you wish to enter into life, keep the commandments." He asked him, "Which ones?" And Jesus replied, "'You shall not kill; you shall not commit adultery; you shall not steal; you shall not bear false witness; honor your father and your mother'; and 'you shall love your neighbor as yourself.'" The young man said to him, "All of these I have observed. What do I still lack?" Jesus said to him, "If you wish to be perfect, go, sell what you have and give to the poor, and you will have treasure in heaven. Then come, follow me." When the young man heard this statement, he went away sad, for he had many possessions. And Jesus said to his disciples, "Amen, I say to you, it will be hard for one who is rich to enter the kingdom of heaven. Again I say to you, it is easier for a camel to pass through the eye of a needle than for one who is rich to enter the kingdom of God."

The Rich Young Man
Matthew 19:16–24

The Solution

As hinted all along, the unique and radical solution elucidated herein is the love of **Jesus Christ**, the salvation of God, who extended His arms on a cross, $\mathbf{Y} = \mathbf{X}$, crowned by the thorns of our cascading transgressions. He is "the way, the truth, and the life" (Jn 14:6); the unity of perfect love (Jn 10:30), $\mathbf{1} = \mathbf{0.999}\ldots$, always positive and merciful; the announced Prince of Peace (Is 9:5); our shelter from the *wind* (Is 32:2); the one calling us to the narrow gate (*point*) (Mt 7:13), commanding us to forgive (seventy times seven times, as portrayed on the second level of the uneven cascade) (Mt 18:22), and inviting us to be recognized by our love (Jn 13:35); and the one by which there is eternal life (Jn 3:16).

Yes, the enemy is the devil, the ancient serpent (Gn 3:1–5); the father of lies (Jn 8:44); $\mathbf{2/3} = \mathbf{0.666}\ldots$, always negative for "there is not truth in him at all" (Jn 8:44); "the ruler of the power of the air" (Eph 2:2) who, opposite to Jesus, scatters us with his turbulent wind (Mt 12:30); "the ruler of the world" (Jn 12:31), forever eating *dust* (Is 65:25); and the defeated murderer that shall be "blown out" when Jesus returns (2 Thes 2:8).

The symbols here are universal as they reflect our choices: truth vs. lies, light vs. darkness, and life vs. death. As exemplified by the Apostle Peter, who denied Jesus three times before the cock crowed twice, $\mathbf{2/3} = \mathbf{0.666}\ldots$, (Mk 14:66–72) and who later on acknowledged him three times, $\mathbf{1} = \mathbf{0.999}\ldots$, (Jn 21:15–17), we are called to remain in Jesus' love (Jn 15:7) (and not just three times!) and be guided by the **Spirit of Truth** (Jn 16:12) so that we may arrive to the **Father** (Jn 14:6), the **Origin**. For, poignantly, when He was crucified, there was *darkness* from the **6**th to the **9**th hour; He died at the **9**th hour (Mk 15:33–37); and the veil in the temple was torn down by the *middle* (Lk 23:45) to unveil God's perfect solution for us all: the balanced and solid **fifty-fifty** condition we may taste by freely **loving** God and one another.[37]

The Hypotenuse

By the wisdom of science
simply divides the air,
to dissipate all its heat
coding a subtle cascade.

Turbulence is selfish game
for it scatters the whole,
and its sequence is a frame
for the options of the world.

Two options before us
two pathways ahead,
the one is the longest
the other straight.

We journey directly
or go by the legs,
we follow intently
or end up in pain.

By walking the flatness
or hiking the spikes,
we travel in lightness
or take serious frights.

The incentive is unity
and the call proportion,
the key is forgiveness
and the goal true notion.

In wandering wickedness
there is never fruit,
but in ample humbleness
one encounters the root.

There is no excuse,
oh listen my friend:
it's by the hypotenuse
or else by the legs.

There is no solution
but walking straight:
the spikes of disorder
insinuate the way.

There is a best pathway,
the palpably smooth.
It's by the hypotenuse
and walking in truth.

There is one solution,
I tell you the truth.
It's by the hypotenuse
and walking in truth.

For any other pathway
will lead us astray.
It's by the hypotenuse,
there is no other way.

Oh listen, you brother,
let's brighten the day.
It's by the hypotenuse,
there is no other way.

Otherwise, the devil
shall pull by the legs.
It's by the hypotenuse
or else by the legs.

For such road is fractured,
as long as it gets.
**It's by the hypotenuse
or else by the legs.**

Oh let's mend the broken,
growing to the root.
**It's by the hypotenuse,
the one that yields fruit.**

Let's keep equilibrium,
avoiding dark soot.
**It's by the hypotenuse,
the one that yields fruit.**

Oh listen, you sister,
a counsel from science.
**It's by the hypotenuse:
the simplest design.**

I tell you integrating,
don't leave it to chance.
**It's by the hypotenuse:
the simplest design.**

**It's by the hypotenuse:
the simplest design...**

609

Six, zero, nine, a dear song
numbers unfolding daylong,
six, zero, nine, a clean gong
symbols inviting us to love.

From six to six
revolving inwards,
from six to six
I went downwards.

From six to six
dividing selfishly,
from six to six
lying endlessly.

From six to six
trying to be a rose,
from six to six
being only a nasty thorn.

Six, zero, nine, a dear song
numbers unfolding daylong,
six, zero, nine, a clean gong
symbols inviting us to love.

From six to zero
I tapered my speed,
from six to zero
the tempest did not lead.

From six to zero
I no longer postponed,
from six to zero
I finally atoned.

From six to zero
I experienced peace,
from six to zero
my loneliness ceased.

**Six, zero, nine, a dear song
numbers unfolding daylong,
six, zero, nine, a clean gong
symbols inviting us to love.**

From zero to nine
the spiral turned over,
from zero to nine
I dared to love others.

From zero to nine
I attempted prayers,
from zero to nine
I became a repairer.

From zero to nine
infinity flowed free,
from zero to nine
unity grew in me.

**Six, zero, nine, a dear song
numbers unfolding daylong,
six, zero, nine, a clean gong
symbols inviting us to love.**

From nine to nine
weaving my reality,
from nine to nine
dreaming its totality.

From nine to nine
conquering my greed,
from nine to nine
planting a new seed.

From nine to nine
despite a clear spite,
from nine to nine
knowing there is light.

**Six, zero, nine, a dear song
numbers unfolding daylong,
six, zero, nine, a clean gong
symbols inviting us to love.**

Y = X

Y = X
is justice that illuminates,
is balance that fascinates:
Y = X.

Y = X
is the practical alliance,
is the precious reliance:
Y = X.

Y = X
is true word that matures,
is a spiral that endures:
Y = X.

Y = X
is the spotless resting place,
is the state of mighty grace:
Y = X.

Y = X
is smoothness that esteems,
is a lovely dove that gleams:
Y = X.

Y = X
is the short and precise root,
is the weaving of the truth:
Y = X.

Y = X
is a future that forgives,
is crowned science that is:
Y = X.

Y = X
is the ever tender tune,
is an impartial tribune:
Y = X.

Y = X
is all innocence that heeds,
is a garden with no weeds:
Y = X.

Y = X
is the simple clear sign,
is the majestic design:
Y = X.

Y = X
is brotherhood that heals,
is diversity that shields:
Y = X.

Y = X
is the real chaste embrace,
is the goodness of a yes:
Y = X.

Y = X
is a smile that edifies,
is a spin that rectifies:
Y = X.

Y = X
is all gentleness in us,
is the everlasting plus:
Y = X.

Y = X
is inspiration that calls,
is growing to be small:
Y = X.

Y = X
is the forgotten territory,
is the improbable story:
Y = X.

Y = X
is revelation that nests,
is surrendering the rest:
Y = X.

Y = X
is the dustless short incline,
is the faithful narrow line:
Y = X.

Y = X
is renouncing all spears,
is experiencing no fears:
Y = X.

Y = X
is the perennial giveaway,
is pure life with no decay:
Y = X.

Y = X
is the only perfect remedy,
is loving, even the enemy:
Y = X.

Acknowledgments

This work could not have been possible without the ample feedback I have received while sharing the message of the hypotenuse at conferences, courses, and impromptu gatherings. I am grateful for the generous support I have received from my students and peers at the University of California and from my friends and colleagues worldwide.

The ideas herein have been clarified via a web of exquisite conversations with Marta, Cristina & Mariana Puente, Carlos & Constanza Puente, Patricia Puente, Juan Carlos & Ilea de Zubiría, Mario, Xiomara, Andrés Camilo & Silvia María Díaz-Granados, Enrique, Gloria, Jorge & Fernando Juliao, Julio & Cristina Puente, Steve Bennett, Germán Vives, Carolina Durán, Mike Tansey, Joe Wheaton, Camilo Bernal, Andrew Coffey, Richard Blinn, Bellie Sivakumar, Jorge Pinzón, María Isabel Escobar, Nelson Obregón, Andrea Cortis, Carlos Rueda, Akin Orhun, Nels Ruud, José Constantine, Jan Fleckenstein, Fariba Sirjani, Richard Bruce, Karen Bordigon, Mark Grismer, Thomas Bui, Martha Vanzina, Walter & Lucy Duque, Fernando Duarte, Luis Sánchez, María José Berenguer, Jairo Uribe, Carlos Molina, Ramón Llamas, Marc Parlange, Verne Scott, Thomas Harter, Joe Stasulat, Barry Gan, Keith Beven, Vit Klemeš, P. K. Bhattacharya, David Dionisi, Steve Grattan, Wes Wallender, Gerhard Epke, Huai-Hsien Huang, and Julia-Rose Padilla, among others.

The lovely artwork of Fernando Duarte and Huai-Hsien Huang and the brotherly encouragement of Steve Bennett are greatly appreciated.

Notes

1. The dynamics involved may be easily followed molding a bar of modeling clay while maintaining its width constant. If the height of the original bar is one unit, the two rectangles shown, having length $1/2$ and areas 0.7 and 0.3 respectively, have heights of 1.4 and 0.6 vertical units. This is so, for the area of the rectangle is the product of the base times its height.

2. The areas of the four rectangles correspond to the familiar expansion of $(p+q)^2$, that is, p^2, plus twice pq, plus q^2, where $p = 70\%$ and $q = 30\%$. As these rectangles have equal lengths of one quarter, their heights are, from left to right, $4p^2$, $4pq$, $4pq$, and $4q^2$.

3. The eight rectangles shown have areas given by the expansion of $(p + q)^3$. The four layers defined by the areas p^3, p^2q, pq^2, and q^3, happen, in order, once, three times, three times, and once. Notice how, unlike the previous level, the rectangles no longer are arranged from tallest to smallest, for the two intermediate layers intertwine.

4. This *multiplicative cascade* clearly happens in powers of 2. When it is carried for n levels, it generates 2^n rectangles of equal length $1/2^n$, whose areas are given by the expansion of $(p+q)^n$. This yields $(n + 1)$ finely intertwined layers p^n, $p^{n-1}q, \ldots, q^n$, that happen according to the celebrated Pascal's triangle:

$$
\begin{array}{ccccccccc}
 & & & & 1 & & & & \\
 & & & 1 & & 1 & & & \\
 & & 1 & & 2 & & 1 & & \\
 & 1 & & 3 & & 3 & & 1 & \\
1 & & 4 & & 6 & & 4 & & 1 \\
 & & & & \vdots & & & &
\end{array}
$$

For lucid reviews of Pascal's triangle and the multiplicative cascade, the reader is referred to H.-O. Peitgen, H. Jürgens, and D.

Saupe, *Chaos and Fractals, New Frontiers of Science,* Springer-Verlag, 1992 and J. Feder, *Fractals,* Plenum Press, 1988.

5. As the largest area after n levels is p^n and as such a rectangle has length $1/2^n$, its height is $(2p)^n$. This quantity gives 56.69 when $p = 0.7$ and $n = 12$.

6. This fact may be easily verified using Pascal's triangle as explained in note 4, as follows. When $n = 16$, the top 7 layers are made of $1 + 16 + 120 + 560 + 1,820 + 4,368 + 8,008 = 14,893$ rectangles, which is, dividing by $2^{16} = 65,536$, 22.7% of the population. These rectangles have a total area of $(0.7)^{16} + 16 \cdot (0.7)^{15}(0.3) + 120 \cdot (0.7)^{14}(0.3)^2 + 560 \cdot (0.7)^{13}(0.3)^3 + 1,820 \cdot (0.7)^{12}(0.3)^4 + 4,368 \cdot (0.7)^{11}(0.3)^5 + 8,008 \cdot (0.7)^10(0.3)^4 = 0.825 = 82.5\%$ of the wealth.

7. This construction may also be easily followed molding a bar of modeling clay. At this stage, the two rectangles shown, having area $1/2$ and length $1/3$, have a height of $3/2$ vertical units.

8. The diagram uses the same hole proportions, that is, one-third of one-third (one-ninth) on the second level, one-third of one-ninth (one-twenty-seventh) on the third level, and so on. Clearly, this multiplicative cascade also happens in powers of two. When it is carried for n levels, it generates 2^n non-contiguous rectangles with area $1/2^n$, whose common lengths and heights are $1/3^n$ and $(3/2)^n$, respectively.

9. The set of disjoint points in which the (infinite) spikes ultimately concentrate is known as the (triadic) *Cantor set,* after German mathematician George Cantor who introduced it in 1883. This set, also known as *Cantor dust* due to its utter lack of cohesion, is a prototypical **fractal** set, as found in many applications ranging from physics to economics and to biology.

For an elegant and fun introduction to fractals, the reader is referred to N. Lesmoir-Gordon, W. Rood, R. Edney, *Introducing Fractal Geometry,* Totem Books, 2000. For a complete treatment of the subject the reader is referred to B. B. Mandelbrot, *The Fractal Geometry of Nature,* W. H. Freeman, 1982.

10. Following note 8, the common height after twelve levels is $(3/2)^{12} = 129.75$.

11. The distributions of wealth and income throughout the world are known to be rather skewed. Indeed as it can be easily verified, interpolation of the values given by the first cascade when $n = 20$ and $p = 0.7$, as defined in note 4 and as done in note 6, closely fit the wealth of the richest 5, 10, 20, and 40% in the **United States** as reported in 1998, that is, in order, 59 (57), 71 (70), 84 (84), and 95% (95) of the resources, with the cascade values given in parenthesis. However, the wealth of the richest 1% is underestimated by the cascade, 38% (30).

Wealth distributions of countries throughout the world may be fitted via more general multiplicative cascades leading to thorns and dust. These may be obtained splitting the mass in more than two pieces (if needed) and selecting possibly distinct multipliers from level to level, as required. This framework certainly fits any wealth distribution having an arbitrary Gini index between 0 and 1 as defined in economics, where 0 denotes equality and 1 the concentration of wealth in a single individual.

For relevant statistics on wealth distributions around the world, the reader is referred to K. Phillips, *Wealth and Democracy,* Broadway Books, 2002; L. A. Keister, *Wealth in America,* Cambridge University Press, 2000; J. D. Sachs, *The End of Poverty,* The Penguin Press, 2005; and to the web site *www.globalpolicy.org.*

12. For lucid accounts on the state of democratic ideas in our world, the reader is referred to V. Klemeš, *An Imperfect Fit,* Trafford, 2003; E. F. Schumacher, *Small is Beautiful,* Blond & Briggs Ltd, 1973; and J. Wallis, *God's Politics,* Harper San Francisco, 2005; and to references therein.

13. The sets of thorns from the first cascade corresponding to a given height have the same non-contiguous (fractal) structure of the second cascade, but their dusts have variable sparseness from layer to layer. Their densities, defined by couples via Pascal's triangle, are recovered varying the hole size on the second cascade from

one-third to a generic value h, with denser layers corresponding to smaller hole sizes and vice versa.

These observations show why the two cascades, that is, the two lies, are, in the end, **intimately related to one another** and explain why the outcome of the first one is known as a *multifractal*. For additional information on multifractals, the reader is referred to J. Feder, *Fractals*, Plenum Press, 1988 and M. Schroeder, *Fractals, Chaos, Power Laws*, W. H. Freeman, 1991.

14. Although the cascade ideas do not explicitly capture the dynamics of wealth accumulation but rather snapshots at given times (cf. note 11) and not diminishing the improvements in standards of living brought up by technological advances, the uneven cascade can be used, even if only metaphorically, to model the further fragmentation and ample dusts (fractals) that would inevitably happen should imbalances persist. For instance, if $p = 0.7$ and $n = 30$, the richest 5, 10, and 20% on such a society would have, in order, 73, 84, and 92% of the wealth, a considerable increase from 57, 70, and 84, as reported in note 11 when $n = 20$. If $p = 0.75$ and $n = 30$, the (ever-intertwined) disparities are even worse as they give, for the same percentiles, in order, 90, 95, and 98% of the wealth.

For more on the thorny subject of globalization, the reader is referred to N. Hertz, *Silent Takeover: Global Capitalism and the Death of Democracy*, Free Press, 2002 and T. H. Friedman, *The Lexus and the Olive Tree: Understanding Globalization*, Anchor Books, 2000.

15. As the thorns ultimately concentrate in dust, there are indeed plateaus everywhere. The length of such horizontal portions, L_h, is certainly **one** unit, for the length of the holes

$$L_h = 1/3 + 2 \cdot 1/9 + 4 \cdot 1/27 + \ldots,$$

gives a geometric series

$$L_h = 1/3 \cdot \sum_{n=0}^{\infty} (2/3)^n = 1/3 \cdot \frac{1}{1 - 2/3} = 1.$$

If the person parachuting on the landscape is sufficiently "small" in size, he or she would then land on a plateau.

16. There are lines on the diagram that appear to be inclined, but this is just an optical illusion due to the resolution of the graph. Ultimately, all lines are either horizontal or vertical, and hence the length of the boundary equals **two** units.

17. The devil's staircase was so named by George Cantor in 1883. The propagation of any hole, no matter how small, and irrespective of placement within the original bar, clearly yields thorns over dust, plateaus everywhere, and hence a devil's staircase.

18. The shown cloud of dust (and any other given by the condition $p \neq 1/2$) is a mathematical "monster," being a continuous curve with no derivatives anywhere. As $p = 0.7$ and $q = 0.3$ are both less than one, the generic value (mass) of a thorn, i.e., $p^k q^j$, tends to **zero** when $k + j$ tend to infinity, and hence the boundary is locally flat everywhere, for "nothing" is being added at any given point.

That the first cascade is not the lesser evil can also be understood recalling that the second lie, yielding devil's staircases, is present on all the thorny layers grown by the first lie (cf. note 13).

19. If one parachutes on the hypotenuse, one slides into the origin!

20. This particular analogy in regards to our actions is, of course, not entirely precise, for we hardly break equilibrium by exactly the same path. However, combining the cascades helps us visualize the dreadful consequences of our "imbalances" and "holes," for the implied patterns containing thorns and dust sadly reflect our empty hearts, broken relations, disjoint societies, violence, and war.

21. The cascade model for turbulence was first proposed by British physicist and pacifist Lewis Fry Richardson in 1922.

22. Technically, fully developed turbulence happens when the *Reynolds* number, $Re = \frac{v \cdot L}{\nu}$, is sufficiently large (say, greater than 200), that is, when the inertia given by v times L, the product of velocity and a characteristic length, vastly overpowers the air's viscosity ν.

Such a condition happens commonly in the atmosphere when the velocity exceeds 15 miles per hour.

For further details on the nature of turbulence, the reader is referred to U. Frish, *Turbulence,* Cambridge University Press, 1995.

23. As first reported by C. Meneveau and K. Sreenivasan, "Simple multifractal cascade model for fully developed turbulence," *Physical Review Letters,* 59:1424, 1987, one-dimensional observations of atmospheric turbulence, and other flows gathered in the laboratory, are **universally** consistent with a reordering of the thorns produced by the first cascade when p is precisely 70%. Remarkably, nature yields, from Afghanistan to Zimbabwe, spikes arranged according to Pascal's triangle, but the process is unpredictable, for the largest offspring eddies (containing 70%) do not happen always to the left but rather appear either left or right, guided by chance.

24. Notwithstanding the distinct orientation of eddies depending on the northern or southern hemispheres, it is curious to note that the fraction 2/3, depicting geometrically the **inward** motion of successive eddies, is found prominently in various results pertaining to turbulence. They include the "two-thirds" law, which says that squared variations of velocities at two locations within a flow are related to their separation raised to the power 2/3 and that 2/3 is the proper value for the two free parameters of a state-of-the-art random cascade model that generalizes the one explained herein.

For further details, the reader is referred to Z. S. She and E. C. Waymire, "Quantized energy cascade and log-Poisson statistics in fully developed turbulence," *Physical Review Letters,* 74:262, 1995 and U. Frish, *Turbulence,* Cambridge University Press, 1995.

25. Coincidentally, "the poor in developing and former communist countries constitute two-thirds of the world's population," H. de Soto, *The Mystery of Capital,* Basic Books, p. 74, 2000.

26. The small scale η at which dissipation happens depends on the Reynolds number, Re, and the initial scale of the system, L_0, as $\eta/L_0 = Re^{-3/2}$. This condition determines the number of cascade

levels to dissipation, n, from the equation $Re^{-3/2} \approx 1/2^n$, which yields $n = 12$ for $Re = 256$ and $n = 24$ for $Re = 65,536$.

27. To reverse the downward spiral of turbulence, the Reynolds number ought to be small. This means lowering the "velocities in our lives," diminishing our "characteristic lengths," and augmenting our "viscosities."

28. This fact may be easily proven. Calling $x = 0.999\ldots$, yields $10x = 9.999\ldots$. Then subtracting these two quantities gives the simple equation $9x = 9$, which gives $0.999\ldots = 1$.

29. The nature of the two generic spirals may be further appreciated from their expressions in polar coordinates. While the **natural** one is, just by convention in mathematics, $r = e^{-\theta}$, with r denoting a distance from the origin and θ representing the (counterclockwise) angle from the positive x axis, the **loving** one is $r = e^{\theta} = e^{+\theta}$, where the positive is often taken for granted.

30. As there is eventual dissipation on a turbulent cascade, there is darkness whenever selfish eddies persist. This condition is avoided only when the positive spiral reigns.

31. These curious observations can be visualized by superimposing the two spirals on a clock and noticing that the negative spiral travels a finite length as it goes to its center while the positive one goes out forever.

For more on exponential functions, the reader is referred to E. Maor, *e. The Story of a Number,* Princeton University Press, 1994.

32. As a natural cascade cannot be sustained forever (cf. note 26), the laws of physics suggest that it is wise to deliberately reverse the universal "pyramid scheme" embedded in the winning cascade in order to avoid global dissipation (cf. note 14). For even if we do not know the value of the "Reynolds number of the world," injustice and terrorism cannot be prevented by a selfish market alone, but by the bold sharing of natural and human resources between "rich" and "poor" peoples and nations.

33. Notice how the slogans "the people united will never be defeated," "united we stand," and "we are number one" are satisfied only in the "root of equilibrium."

34. As we all realize it, there is a real axis of evil passing through the hearts of every single one of us, so it is up to each one of us to do our part. Interestingly, letting go of our (superior or inferior) postures leads us, just by the effect of "gravity," to the best destination. For the implied surface, although flat in the limit, has a convex-up shape for a finite number of levels that guarantees finding the improbable point.

35. These observations are seen in the imaginary number $i = \sqrt{-1}$, and in the simple equation (in Roman numerals) $I = +\sqrt{+1}$. The difference between the little i and the truthful I is particularly meaningful in English!

36. The most economic condition is potently symbolized by the cohesive level zero on both cascades. Strikingly, $(p+q)^0 = 1$ and hence **zero** (no more lies) denotes the required power of self-sacrifice leading us to **unity**:

$$\text{🧍} = 0.999... = 1$$

37. Curiously, there is no distinction between those who belong to the 99% and those to the 1%, as God's universal mercy is witnessed in Jesus' parable of the lost sheep: "What is your opinion? If a man has a hundred sheep and one of them goes astray, will he not leave the ninety-nine in the hills and go in search of the stray? And if he finds it, amen, I say to you, he rejoices more over it than over the ninety-nine that did not stray." (Mt 18:12–13)

Index